This Book Belongs To

_____

_____

_____

Cover and text design by Suzanne Morgan
Illustrations by Patricia Frevert

Sunday and Every Day

My Little Book of Unitarian Universalism

Patricia Frevert, Editor

Skinner House Books
Boston

Contents

Chalice Lightings   3

Our Seven Principles   9

The Six Sources of Our Faith   19

Music   27

Table Graces   33

Prayers for Any Day   39

Prayers of Your Own   45

How Unitarian Universalism Began   53

Stories of Unitarian Universalism   57

So many things happen in a Unitarian Universalist congregation! You get to be with old friends and meet new ones. Maybe you will light the chalice, have fun coloring a mural, or join with other kids in a project that helps people in need. This small book is just for you—whether you have been coming to church for a long time or you're just visiting. Here are prayers, songs, and stories to show you a little bit of what your congregation is all about.

Chalice Lightings

We light the chalice as worship begins. It quiets us and reminds us of the reasons we are gathered together. Sometimes we say special words as we light the chalice.

We light this candle to remind ourselves to treat all people kindly because they are our brothers and sisters.

We light this candle to remind ourselves to take good care of the earth, because it is our home.

We light this candle to remind ourselves to live lives full of goodness and love, because that is how we will become the best we can be.

—Anonymous

We light our flaming chalice today for the place of quietness and holiness within each of us, and for whatever helps us to feel peaceful inside.

—Ann Fields and Joan Goodwin

We come together
(bring hands together and clasp them in front of you)
To remind ourselves
(touch your index and middle fingers to your temple)
To treat all people kindly
(spread arms wide, encircling)
Because they are our brothers and sisters,
(fold your arms across your chest, in a hug)
To take good care of the earth,
(raise your arms above your head, in a circle)
Because it is our home,
(fold your arms, holding your elbows, and motion as though rocking a baby)
To live lives full of goodness and love,
(put both hands over your heart)
Because that is how we will make
our world
(raise your arms above your head, in a circle)
The best place it can be.
(clap your hands quietly)

—Patty Collins

Life is a gift for which we are grateful.
We gather in community to celebrate the
glories and the mysteries of this great gift.

—MARJORIE MONTGOMERY

We are Unitarian Universalists
With minds that think,
Hearts that love,
And hands that are ready to serve.
Together we care for our Earth
And work for friendship and peace in
   our world.

—AISHA HAUSER AND SUSAN LAWRENCE

Glory be to the earth and the wind.
Glory be to the sun and the rain.
Glory be to animals and children
   and women and men.
Glory be to our holy flame
   which calls us together as one.

—BETTYE A. DOTY

We light this chalice
To bring friendship and love,
To think of others less fortunate than us,
And to remember the time before
  religious freedom.

—South Nassau Unitarian Church,
  Freeport, New York

We light this chalice for the light
  of truth.
We light this chalice for the warmth
  of love.
We light this chalice for the energy
  of action.

—Mary Ann Moore

Our Seven Principles

Our Principles help us to be the best people we can be. Our Principles are the promises that Unitarian Universalists make to one another.

We believe that each and every person is important.

May I be safe
May I be happy
May I be well
May I live in peace

May you be safe
May you be happy
May you be well
May you live in peace

—BUDDHIST PRAYER,
    ADAPTED BY SUSAN FREUDENTHAL

2

We believe that all people should be treated fairly.

Let us bless and keep one another.
Let kindness rule in our hearts
and compassion in our lives,
until we meet again.
Amen.

—JOHN MORGAN

3

We believe that our churches are places where all people are accepted, and where we keep on learning together.

May I know the circle of love
into which I was born.
May my life make the circle
wider and wider,
starting with my family and
    these friends,
starting today.

—Betsy Darr

We believe that each person must be free to search for what is true and right in life.

Search and search again
without losing hope;
You may find sometime
a treasure on your way.

—MUHAMMAD IQBAL

We believe that all people should have a voice and a vote about the things that concern them.

May words I say be fair and true
May love be a guide in all I do
May kindness sing within my heart
And may peace be with us while
   we're apart.

—BERYL ASCHENBERG

We believe that we should work for a peaceful, fair and free world.

I offer you peace.
I offer you love.
I offer you friendship.
I see your beauty.
I hear your need.
I feel your feelings.
My wisdom flows from the Highest
   Source.
I salute that Source in you.
Let us work together for unity and love.

—Mohandas Gandhi

We believe that we should care for our planet earth.

From our hearts,
(put both hands over your heart)
with our hands,
(open your arms wide)
for the earth,
(cup your hands together as if you are holding a small ball)
all the world together.
(cross your hands over your heart, then raise your arms and open them wide)

—Children of the Green Earth Pledge

The Six Sources
of Our Faith

Where do we look for wisdom? So many places! Throughout the ages, people all over the world have had wise things to say. We grow in wisdom as we learn from our parents, our teachers, and our own everyday experiences.

We celebrate the sense of wonder we all share.

Touch the earth, reach the sky!
Walk on shores while spirits fly
over the ocean, over the land,
our faith a quest to understand.

Touch the earth, reach the sky!
Hug the laughter, feel the cry.
May we see where we can give,
for this is what it means to live.

Touch the earth, reach the sky!
Soar with courage ever high;
spirits joining as we fly,
to touch the earth, to reach the sky.

—GRACE LEWIS-McLAREN

2

We learn from people who are kind and fair.

Parents are teachers,
Friends are teachers,
Sisters are teachers too;
Grandmas are teachers, grandpas
   are teachers
And you're a teacher too!

—Kathi Rosen

We learn from the wisdom of other religions.

Grandfather Great Spirit
Fill us with the light
Give us the strength to understand and
    the eyes to see.
Teach us to walk the soft earth
    as relatives
To all that live.

—Sioux prayer

We honor the Christian and Jewish teachings that ask us to love all others as we love ourselves.

God be in my head
   and in my understanding.
God be in my eyes
   and in my looking.
God be in my mouth
   and in my speaking.
God be in my heart
   and in my thinking.
God be at my end
   and in my departing.

—SARUM PRIMER

We believe in the use of reason and the discoveries of science.

Books to the ceiling,
Books to the sky,
My pile of books is a mile high.
How I love them! How I need them!
I'll have a long beard by the time
    I read them.

—Arnold Lobel

We are part of the harmony of nature and the sacred circle of life.

Where I sit is holy,
Holy is the ground.
Forest, mountain, river
Listen to the sound.
Great Spirit circle
All around me.

—Blackfoot chant

Music

Singing is fun! It feels good to sing with other people, like we do in church. You can find these two songs in the Unitarian Universalist hymnbook *Singing the Living Tradition*.

Spirit of Life

Words and music by Carolyn McDade

From You I Receive

From you I re - ceive,_____ to you I give,_____ to - geth-er_____ we share, and from this we live.

Words and music by Joseph and Nathan Segal

Table Graces

Words of thanks can begin a family meal or a community dinner. You can say words like the table graces on these pages or make up one of your own. Sometimes we like to say grace together. Other times a leader says the words as we listen.

God, we thank you for this food,
for rest and home and all things good,
for wind and rain and sun above,
but most of all, for those we love.

—ANONYMOUS

Earth, who gives to us this food,
Sun, who makes it ripe and good,
Dear Earth, dear Sun, by you we live.
To you our loving thanks we give.

—ANONYMOUS

Goddess, bless this food you have
    given me.
Let it be filled with your divine energy
So that I will be healthy
And live a long and happy life.
Goddess bless! Blessed be!

—SIRONA KNIGHT

A circle of friends is a blessed thing.
Sweet is the breaking of bread
   with friends.
For the honor of their presence at our table
We are deeply grateful.
Amen.

—ANONYMOUS

Loving Spirit,
Be our guest,
Dine with us,
Share our bread,
That our table
Might be blessed
And our souls be fed.

—GARY KOWALSKI

Let us bless the source of life
that brings forth bread from the earth.

—JEWISH BLESSING

Blessed art Thou,
O Lord our God,
King of the Universe,
who creates many living
beings and the things they
need. For all that Thou hast
created to sustain
the life of every living
being, blessed be Thou,
the Life of the Universe.

—Jewish grace

The silver rain, the shining sun,
The fields where scarlet poppies run,
And all the ripples of the wheat
Are in the foods that we do eat.
So when we sit for every meal and
Say our grace, we always feel
That we are eating rain and sun
And fields where scarlet poppies run.

—Shaker grace

Bless our food,
Bless our friends,
Come, Spirit, be with us.
May our hearts fill with peace,
Let your presence surround us.
Spirit of Love may you bloom and grow,
Bloom and grow forever.
Bless our food,
Bless our friends,
Bless our lives forever.

—JAN EVANS-TILLER

Prayers for Any Day

A prayer can be a wish, a promise, or a way to say how you feel. Some people think of prayer as talking with God, and others think of it as a way of naming what is most important to them. You can pray alone or with others, out loud or silently.

Peace be to this house
And to all who live in it.
Peace be to the people who enter
And to those who depart.

—Traditional

Dear God,
May I be kind,
Strong and brave,
Joyful, useful, loving,
Honest and healthy.

—Meg Barnhouse

The moon shines bright,
The stars give light
Before the break of day;
God bless you all
Both great and small
And send you a joyful day.

—Traditional

I see the moon,
And the moon sees me.
God bless the moon,
And God bless me.

—Traditional

Now I lay me down to sleep
And float into God's dreamy deep.
For my life my thanks I give.
To love the world, for this I live.
When I wake in the morning light,
May God be with me and guide my sight.

—Susan Maginn and Peter Campbell

Blest be the hand that plants the seed,
Blest be the Earth giving all that we need.
Blest be the food we share among friends,
Blest be the love that knows no end.

—Joyce Poley

Spirits of the Earth and Sky,
Help me understand just why
Not all bodies are the same.
I know that no one is to blame,

But I fear being left behind.
Help all others keep in mind
That we can differ: slow and fast,
Tall and short, first and last.

—Eliza Blanchard, adapted

I praise the blue sky.
I praise the sun that is in you.
I praise the bright moon.
I praise the shining stars in you.

—Anonymous

On your birthday we pray
Green be the grass you walk on,
Blue be the skies above you,
Pure be the joys that surround you,
True be the hearts that love you.

—Irish blessing

Good night! Good night!
Far flies the light;
But still God's love
Shall flame above,
Making all bright.
Good night! Good night!

—Victor Hugo

Bless this house, which is our home.
May we welcome all who come.

—Anonymous

The breeze at dawn has secrets to
    tell you.
Don't go back to sleep.
You must ask for what you really want.
Don't go back to sleep.
People are going back and forth across
    the doorsill
where the two worlds touch.
The door is round and open.
Don't go back to sleep.

—Rumi, translated by Coleman Barks

Prayers of Your Own

You can make up your own prayers. Your prayer can be about anything you want. The words are up to you. Here are prayers that were written by children, and a bedtime prayer that you can create for yourself.

For drawing and writing,
  and playing guitar
For showing off magic, for climbing a tree
We join our voices in thanks!

For tennis and soccer, scoring goals
  and home runs
Bicycles, unicycles, kayaks and skates
We join our voices in thanks!

For technology, fireworks, ice cubes,
  and trains
For learning to dance, for our bones
  and our brain
We join our voices in thanks!

For eating and sleeping, clean water
  and food
For relatives, friends, my church
  and my school
We join our voices in thanks!

—CHILDREN OF NORTH PARISH IN
  NORTH ANDOVER, MA

I love you, Big World
I wish I could call you
And tell you a secret
That I love you, World.

—P. WOLLNER, AGE 7

Let everything that has breath
Praise the Lord.
The donkeys stampede on their feet,
The owls hoo,
The roosters cock-a-doodle-doo
And flap their wings,
The tigers roar,
The snakes rattle,
And the ducks quack and flap.
Let everything that has breath
Talk to the Lord
And praise Him.

—ISAAC CARUSO, AGE 6

Bless my parents and give them health.
Take very, very good care of them,
just like they take care of me.

—Chelsea, age 8

There is an umbrella
In the sky,
It must be raining
In Heaven
I have one prayer to say to God
Don't let it rain tomorrow.

—V. Cokeman, age 10

Kindness

A loving arm
Shelters me
From any harm.

The shelteredness
Of kindness
Flows around me.

—M. Flett, age 9

Dios *bendice a los animales*
a los niños enfermos
a las plantas
y gracias por lo que nos das.
Amén.

God bless the animals
and the sick kids
and the plants
and thank you for all that you give us.
Amen.

—GABRIELA, AGE 9

As I curl up and go to sleep
I have such lovely thoughts
The darkness of my room,
The warmness of my bed
And what the day has brought.

—A. GOODMAN, AGE 11

You can make up your own bedtime prayer by adding your own words to finish each sentence.

Tonight I am thankful for _____.

And I am sorry for _____.

Tomorrow I hope for _____.

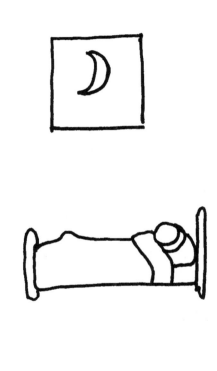

How Unitarian Universalism Began

The beginnings of Unitarian Universalism happened more than two thousand years ago, in the days of the early Christian church.

Unitarian Universalists trace their religious roots back to Jesus, who believed that we should love one another. In 1568, King John Sigismund of Transylvania believed that his people deserved to choose their religion for themselves, and the first Unitarian church was founded there by Francis David. John Murray brought Universalism from England to North America, and then the first Universalist church was formed in Gloucester, Massachusetts, in 1779. Later, in Boston, William Ellery Channing led some ministers to start Unitarianism in America. They formed the American Unitarian Association in 1825.

In many countries and for many generations afterward, Unitarians and Universalists shared their beliefs with others. They believed that every person deserves to be treated with love and respect. They believed that people can think for themselves. They believed that people need to take care of each other and the planet Earth. In 1961, the two faiths united to become Unitarian Universalism.

Do you recognize any of these Unitarians and Universalists?

John Quincy Adams
U.S. president

Louisa May Alcott
author of *Little Women*
and other books

Susan B. Anthony
women's rights leader

Clara Barton
founder of the American
Red Cross

Alexander Graham Bell
inventor of the telephone

Sophia Lyon Fahs
minister and religious
educator

Fannie Farmer
cookbook author

Robert Fulghum
minister and author

Lewis Latimer
scientist

Beatrix Potter
author and artist

Frank Lloyd Wright
architect

Whitney Young
civil rights leader

To learn more about these people, ask your teacher or another adult.

Stories of Unitarian Universalism

Find out about King John of Transylvania, who let his people choose their faith for themselves. Discover why Reverend Čapek created the first Flower Communion. And meet Hans Deutsch, who designed the flaming chalice, a symbol of Unitarian Universalism.

King Sigismund
and Francis David

John Sigismund was a baby when the nobles elected him as their new king. "All hail King John Sigismund of Hungary!" they shouted. But the young king and his mother, Queen Isabella, were not able to defend their small country against outside forces. Soon they ended up ruling just a corner of the former kingdom, a grassy plain surrounded by high mountains. It was called Transylvania.

In Transylvania, the people fought about religion. Catholics argued with Lutherans, Lutherans argued with the Greek Orthodox, the Greek Orthodox argued with the Calvinists, the Calvinists argued with the Catholics. The fighting got worse when the queen died in 1559. King John was just a teenager, and now he was on his own.

"How can we stop the fighting?" King John asked an advisor.

"One king, one country!" the advisor said. "That's what they do in France and Spain. You must choose one religion that everyone will follow. That way, we will have no more fighting in Transylvania."

King John thought it over. He invited preachers from different religions to visit his court and talk about their religion. One of these visitors was Francis David, who explained that he believed God was one being instead of three. Today we call this belief Unitarian. After listening to all the preachers who came to visit, King John decided he agreed with Francis David. In 1569 King John became a Unitarian.

But the young king did not agree with his advisor. He did not think that everyone in Transylvania had to be Unitarian. King John decided his people should be free to choose their faith themselves. He made a new law that promised freedom of religion. The law was called the Edict of Torda.

Now the people of Transylvania were free to choose their faith for themselves. Unitarianism was one of the official religions, one of many.

Transylvania is now part of Romania. The people who live there are still free to choose their own faith. There are eighty thousand Unitarians in Romania today.

The First Flower Communion

Some churches have towers with bells that ring out the hours. Some churches have organs whose mighty sound spills out into the streets. Some have handsome doors of carved wood, or colorful stained glass windows. But in 1923, in Prague, Czechoslovakia, there was a plain church that had none of these things. The church had just four walls, a ceiling, and a floor. The church had a door, a few windows, and some wooden chairs.

But the church had something else. It had people. They came every Sunday and they were the most important part of the church, because without people, a church is just a building.

The minister of this church was Norbert Čapek (sounds like CHAH-peck). He had been the minister for just two years. Every Sunday, the congregation listened to

Reverend Čapek's sermon. They sat quietly in their wooden chairs. Afterward, they talked to one another a little bit, and then they went home. That was all—no music, no candles, no food. Not even coffee or doughnuts.

Reverend Čapek wanted more. He wrote some songs, and the people sang them, but mostly the church went on as before.

Then spring arrived, and Norbert Čapek went out for a stroll. The rains had come and gone, birds were singing, and flowers bloomed everywhere the Reverend looked. In the middle of all that beauty, he got a new idea.

That Sunday, Reverend Čapek asked all the people of the church to bring a flower the next week, a budding branch, even a twig. Each person should bring one, he said.

"What kind?" they asked.

"You choose," he said.

"What color?" they asked.

"Each of you choose what you like."

The next Sunday was the first day of summer, and people came to church with flowers of all kinds. There were yellow daisies and purple roses. There were white lilies and blue asters, dark blue pansies and long branches with pale green leaves. Pink and purple, orange and gold—all these colors and more. The flowers spilled over, filling all the vases they could find.

Years later, many members of the church could still remember what Reverend Čapek said that Sunday.

"We are like these flowers," he said. "Different colors, different ages, different sizes. We are different in so many ways. But each of us is beautiful and important, in our own way. Like these flowers."

Reverend Čapek asked them each to take a flower home, choosing a different flower from the one they brought. And they did.

Reverend Čapek called this event the "Flower Festival." Today many Unitarian Universalist churches call it the "Flower Communion" and celebrate it every spring.

The Flaming Chalice

When there's a war, many people are hurt by the violence. During World War II, soldiers and airplanes were firing guns all over Europe, on the ground and in the air. Members of the Unitarian Service Committee went to Europe to help the refugees.

Dr. Charles Joy was in charge of the committee. Knowing that the refugees spoke many different languages, he wanted a symbol that they all would recognize, no matter what language they spoke. Dr. Joy turned to an artist named Hans Deutsch for help. Deutsch was a refugee, so he knew this was urgent. "We want a symbol that will look official and important, so it will impress the border guards," Dr. Joy explained. "And we want it to stand for the spirit of our work, which is to help and serve."

Hans Deutsch made a sketch of a chalice with a flame, surrounded by a circle. When Dr. Joy saw that sketch, he knew it was exactly what he wanted!

Soon refugees all over Europe came to know and trust the flaming chalice, a symbol of freedom and hope during the long and difficult war.

Years later the Unitarian Universalist Association chose the flaming chalice as its symbol. And today, Unitarian Universalists everywhere light the chalice when they gather for worship.

There are all kinds of Unitarian Universalist chalices. Some are carved out of wood, some are made of glass or metal, and others are molded out of clay. Chalices come in many different shapes and sizes and colors, just like we do. The chalice stands for freedom, service, and hope. It is the symbol of Unitarian Universalism.

print ISBN: 978-1-55896-555-3
eBook ISBN: 978-1-55896-581-2

6 5 4 3 / 20 19 18

Library of Congress Cataloging-in-Publication Data

Sunday and every day : my little book of Unitarian Universalism / edited by Patricia Frevert.
p. cm.
ISBN-13: 978-1-55896-555-3 (pbk. : alk. paper)
ISBN-10: 1-55896-555-6 (pbk. : alk. paper)   1. Unitarian Universalist churches—Juvenile literature. I. Frevert, Patricia.
BX9841.3.S86 2010
289.1'32—dc22

                                    2009036395

The stories "King Sigismund and Francis David" and "The First Flower Communion" are adapted from "A Unitarian King: The Edict of Torda" and "A Plain and Simple Beauty: The Flower Communion," in Janeen K. Grohsmeyer's *A Lamp in Every Corner: Our Unitarian Universalist Storybook*, Boston: Unitarian Universalist Association, 2004.

We gratefully acknowledge permission for the following copyrighted materials: Poem by Isaac Caruso from *Blessing the Animals: Prayers and Ceremonies to Celebrate God's Creatures, Wild and Tame*, © 2006 by Lynn L. Caruso, permission granted by SkyLight Paths Publishing, www.skylightpaths.com; poem by Rumi from *Open Secret: Versions of Rumi* by John Moyne and Coleman Barks, reprinted by permission of Coleman Barks; prayer by Sirona Knight from *Goddess Bless! Divine Affirmations, Prayers and Blessings*, reprinted by permission of author; prayers by Chelsea and Gabriela from *Kids Book of Everyday Prayers*, edited by Catherine Odell and Margaret Savitskas (Loyola Press, 2002), reprinted with permission of Loyola Press, to order copies call 1-800-621-1008 or go to www.loyolapress.com; prayers by M. Flett, V. Cokeham, P. Wollner, and A. Goodman from *Miracles: Poems by Children of the English-Speaking World*, edited by Richard Lewis, reprinted with permission of The Touchstone Center for Children, www.touchstonecenter.net; poem by Arnold Lobel from *Whiskers and Rhymes*, reprinted with permission of Harper-Collins Publishers; "Spirit of Life" reprinted with permission of Carolyn McDade; "From You I Receive" reprinted with permission of Nathan Segal.